W9-BSF-060

See the City

Written by David F. Marx
Illustrated by Cindy Revell

Children's Press®
A Division of Scholastic Inc.
New York • Toronto • London • Auckland • Sydney
Mexico City • New Delhi • Hong Kong
Danbury, Connecticut

For Tabitha, Allan, Amanda, and Connal
—C.R.

Reading Consultants
Linda Cornwell
Coordinator of School Quality and Professional Improvement
(Indiana State Teachers Association)

Katharine A. Kane
Education Consultant
(Retired, San Diego County Office of Education
and San Diego State University)

Library of Congress Cataloging-in-Publication Data
Marx, David F.
    See the city / written by David F. Marx ; illustrated by Cindy Revell.
      p. cm. – (Rookie reader)
    Summary: A boy and his family enjoy the sights of New York City, from cement
sidewalks and ice-skaters in the park to sparkling lights and dancing on a stage.
    ISBN 0-516-22254-6 (lib. bdg.)   0-516-25966-0 (pbk.)
    [1. New York (N.Y.)—Fiction. 2. City and town life—Fiction.] I. Revell, Cindy, ill.
II. Title. III. Series.
PZ7.M36822 Se 2001
[E]—dc21   00-048501

GROLIER
PUBLISHING
2 3 4 5 6 7 8 9 10 R 10 09 08 07 06 05 04 03 02

Cement sidewalks.

See the city.

Ice-skating in the park.

See the city.

Ships on the sea.

See the city.

Sparkling lights.

15

See the city.

17

Dancing on a stage.

See the city.

So long, city!

Word List (18 words)

a	lights	ships
cement	long	sidewalks
city	on	so
dancing	park	sparkling
ice-skating	sea	stage
in	see	the

About the Author

David F. Marx is a children's author and editor who lives in suburban Chicago. He is the author of several other books in the Rookie Reader, Rookie Read-About Geography, and Rookie Read-About Holidays series for Children's Press.

About the Illustrator

Cindy Revell has been drawing ever since she first picked up a crayon. Now she works in acrylics on paper, but it is just as much fun. She loves working in her home studio that she shares with two cats and lots of books, in Alberta, Canada.

Rookie reader® Level A

Emergent

Read these other Rookie Readers® at another reading level:

Game Day
Cari Meister

Get Out of My Chair
Kathy Schulz

So Many Sounds
Dana Meachen Rau

Children's Press

U.S. $4.95
Can. $6.95

ISBN 0-516-25966-0

9 780516 259666

900

SCHOLASTIC